Memento Mori

Ignatius Maximus John and Grace Lalrinpari Hauzel

Published by Gumby Publishers, 2023.

Table of Contents

About The Book

Moments of fleeting beauty, tender whispers of mortality—'Memento Mori' gracefully weaves together the threads of life and death, inviting you on an introspective journey through its poetic pages. In this captivating collection, every verse serves as a gentle reminder that life's fragility is the very essence of its brilliance.

Through vivid imagery and delicate metaphors, the poet and poetess explores the intricate dance between existence and impermanence. Each poem, like a fragile blossom, unveils the profound truths hidden beneath the surface of our everyday experiences. From the ephemeral beauty of a sunset to the quiet whispers of a departing soul, 'Memento Mori' touches upon the essence of what it means to be alive.

With introspection as its guiding force, this anthology gracefully explores the depths of human emotions—the bittersweet ache of loss, the relentless passage of time, and the profound wisdom that arises from embracing our mortality. It is a tender reminder to seize the present moment, to cherish the connections we forge, and to find solace in the impermanent nature of our existence.

'Memento Mori' is not merely a collection of poems; it is a journey that will touch the depths of your soul and leave you pondering the beauty and transience of life. Immerse yourself in its evocative verses, and let the delicate melodies of mortality resonate within your heart.

Grace Lalrinpari Hauzel is an enthusiastic budding writer who has been writing short stories and poetries since she was 6 years old. She manifested her views on life, emphasizing the enigmatic and arduous journey which are often thought provoking. Grace writes about nature, human emotions and divine love, using human love as an allegory. Grace is notorious for being a sleepyhead, most importantly a blithesome person. Her literary skills have gained recognition and have been awarded various awards.

Ignatius Maximus John is a poet who has been writing for decades. His poems are filled with deep emotion and personal experiences that make his work relatable to many people. He writes about love, heartbreak, and the everyday struggles of life. He often writes about his love for the beauty in nature, which makes his work a beautiful read. He has been published in many magazines and journals, and has won many awards for his work.

Preface

Memento Mori is a Latin phrase that translates to "remember you must die." This phrase is a reminder of the inevitability of death and the transience of life. The concept of Memento Mori has been present in various cultures and religions for centuries. It is a reminder to live life to the fullest and to make the most of every moment.

The concept of Memento Mori dates back to ancient Rome, where it was common for generals to have a slave whisper in their ear during their triumphal processions, "Remember, you are mortal." This was a reminder to the victorious general that his success was fleeting and that he too would eventually die. The concept of Memento Mori was also present in Christianity, where it was used as a reminder of the afterlife and the need to prepare for judgment.

In art, Memento Mori is often depicted through imagery such as skulls, hourglasses, and other symbols of death. These images are meant to remind the viewer of their mortality and the need to live life to the fullest. One of the most famous examples of Memento Mori in art is the painting "The Ambassadors" by Hans Holbein the Younger. In this painting, a skull is hidden in the foreground, only visible when viewed from a certain angle. This symbolizes the idea that death is always present, even if we do not see it.

The concept of Memento Mori has also been used in literature. In William Shakespeare's play "Hamlet," the character Hamlet reflects on the inevitability of death, saying, "To be, or not to be, that is the question: Whether 'tis nobler in the mind to suffer The slings and arrows of outrageous fortune, Or to take arms against a sea of troubles And by opposing end them." Hamlet's soliloquy is a reflection on the transience of life and the inevitability of death.

In modern times, the concept of Memento Mori has taken on a new meaning. It is often used as a reminder to live life to the fullest and to make the most of every moment. This is particularly relevant in a world where we are constantly bombarded with distractions and pressures to conform to societal norms. The idea of Memento Mori reminds us that we only have a limited amount of time on this earth and that we should make the most of it.

One way to incorporate the concept of Memento Mori into our lives is through mindfulness practices such as meditation. By focusing on the present moment, we can become more aware of our mortality and the need to make the most of every moment. This can help us to prioritize what is truly important in life and to let go of distractions that do not serve us.

Another way to incorporate the concept of Memento Mori into our lives is through gratitude practices. By expressing gratitude for the people and experiences in our lives, we can become more aware of the preciousness of life. This can help us to appreciate what we have and to make the most of every moment.

The concept of Memento Mori is a reminder of the inevitability of death and the transience of life. It is a reminder to live life to the fullest and to make the most of every moment. Whether through art, literature, or mindfulness practices, we can incorporate the idea of Memento Mori into our lives and use it as a tool for personal growth and self-reflection. By embracing our mortality, we can live more fully and authentically, making the most of the time we have on this earth.

Ignatius Maximus John & Grace Lalrinpari Hauzel

Blessings

Blessings surround us,
In the air, earth and sky too,
Gratitude within.

Divine fingers touch,
Whispering blessings untold,
Joy fills the heart's cup.

Blessed with life itself,
Grateful for each passing breath,
Blessings untold flow.

Grateful

Grateful heart abounds
Simple joys fill every space
Blessed in every way

Gratitude echoes
Amidst life's storms, stands steadfast
Counting blessings, peace.

Gratefulness brings light
Brightens all that surrounds us
Thankful heart, grateful life.

Divine

Eternal radiance,
Divine light of the cosmos,
Guiding us always.

Benevolent force,
Creator of all that's pure,
Love's constant embrace.

Majestic presence,
Endless grace and mercy flows,
Divine, evermore.

Destiny

Destiny awaits,
A path that must be followed,
Unknown journey's end.

Choices we all make,
Leading towards our future,
Swayed by the unknown.

Fate, a subtle force,
Pushing us towards our dreams,
A life we must build.

Fate

Paths intertwined tight
Fate a master of the game
Moving us with might

No control we hold
Destiny's hand we follow
By fate we are sold

Sands of time they fall
Fate's embrace, both great and small
Life's dance, one and all.

Light

Shed light on the dark,
Reveal the truth that's hidden,
Guiding us to peace.

A candle flickers,
Illuminating the night,
Hope for the lost soul.

Shed light on the path,
Revealing new perspectives,
Wisdom to be found.

Flowers

Burst of color bright
Petals dancing in the breeze
Nature's symphony

Tiny blooms await
Emerging from winter's grip
Hope springs forth anew

Flowers of the field
Wild and free, yet so serene
Nature's purest art

Dead

Lifeless and silent,
All the breath and soul gone now.
Death's eternal grip.

Cold embrace of Death,
Final journey into black,
Farewell to the world.

The heartbeat has stopped,
Eyes closed, the end is nigh.
Rest well, dear departed.

Reflections

Reflecting pond still,
Undisturbed by breeze or throng,
Peace within my soul.

Calm surface mirrors,
A world just beyond our reach,
Infinite beauty.

Glass windows reflect,
Dancing light upon the floor,
Memories we keep.

Traitors

A friend turned to foe
A treacherous mind revealed
Betrayal stings deep

Deceit's deadly game
Trickery, lies, and treason
A traitor's own shame

Broken trust, lost hope
Pride and greed lead some astray
Traitors pay the price

Hang-Man

The storm clouds gather,
A chill creeps up from the ground,
Hang-Man waits tonight.

Silent and alone,
Watching from a distance,
Hang-Man bides his time.

Distant screams echo,
Through the darkness of the night,
Hang-Man's work is done.

Plagues

Locusts take the field
Eating up all in their path
Crops wither and die

The Black Death spreads wide
Rats and fleas carry the plague
Death toll ever rising

Pandemic strikes hard
Millions of lives on the line
Isolation, masks

Pray

Thy silent whispers,
Reverent cries from the soul:
Prayers for peace and love.

Hands clasped, eyes closed tight,
Heavenly hopes whispered low,
Divine peace within.

On bended knee, true
Hearts yearning for grace and strength,
In prayer, we find peace.

Eyes

Eyes gleaming like jewels,
Reflecting infinite depths,
Gazing into souls.

Windows to the soul,
Revealing joy and sorrow,
Guiding us through life.

Luminous and bright,
Betraying each emotion,
Eyes never lie.

Love Lost

A flower wilts
Love faded like petals fall
Heart a sea of pain

Memories, echoes
Whispers of a love now lost
Sorrow grips my soul

The fire now quenched
What once burned bright now ashes
Lost love, eternal

Comedown

Glimpse of euphoria,
Comedown crashing like thunder,
Reality bites.

A fleeting high fades,
Leaves me in an abyss now,
Comedown's bitter truth.

Lethargy sets in,
Comedown strips my energy,
Sorrow nestles deep.

Smile

A smile so bright, warm
Spread across cheeks like sunshine
Heart begins to glow

In the darkest days
A smile, a spark of hope, light
Shining path ahead

A smile, a symbol
Of joy, comfort and peace
Simple yet priceless

Written In Blood

Words etched on paper
Tales of horror and despair
Written in life's blood

Quill and ink in hand
Pages turn, revealing truths
Written in blood red

From the heart it flows
Stories of love and longing
Written in blood ink

Death

Fading into night,
Life's fragile beauty revealed,
Death's embrace awaits.

Silent and unknown,
Leaves falling without a sound,
Death's whisper in wind.

No more pain or fear,
Eternal rest and peace found,
Death, release from life.

Breath

Golden sun rises,
Inhale the fresh morning air,
Breath of life renewed.

Soft and gentle breeze,
Inhale and feel the world's calm,
A peaceful reprieve.

Exhale out the pain,
Breath deep, let go of worry,
Stillness now remains.

Season

Leaves turn gold and red,
Birds flock to warmer places,
Autumn is upon us.

Winter frosty kiss,
Snowflakes cover everything,
Silent and serene.

Spring brings new life, hope,
Flowers bloom, birds sing, earth wakes,
Renewal again.

Sleep

Heavy eyelids droop
Slumber slowly welcomes me
Dreams dance, sweet repose

Nesting in my bed
Moonlight softly whispers, "rest"
Slumber comes to me

Raindrops lullaby
Drifting into peaceful sleep
Dawn awaits my dreams

One

One is the first step,
A journey to self-discovery,
Liberating soul.

In the beginning,
One was the only number,
Powerful and pure.

One heart, one spirit,
Together we can achieve,
Hope for a better world.

Eye

An eye, small, wonders
A window to the inside
Reflects the outside

The eye sees it all
Emotions hidden or shown
True sight is within

Deep pools of color
A gaze that pierces the soul
Eyes tell stories old

Open

Doors swing wide open
An invitation to new
Paths, unknown journeys

Open minds and hearts
Embrace diversity's gift
Peace and love abound

Petals unfurling
Blooms open to share beauty
Nature's sweetest gift

Sadness

Tears on my pillow,
Heart heavy with sorrow's weight,
Loneliness prevails.

Grey clouds obscure light,
My tears drop as rain outside,
Sadness envelops.

A heavy heart beats,
Echoing in empty halls,
Longing for solace.

Suicide

Life becomes too much,
A pain that you cannot shake,
Death seems like the cure.
The darkness creeps in,
A shadow that will not fade,
Suicide beckons.
The weight of the world,
Crushing all hope and all light,
Suicide whispers.

Crucify

Nails piercing his flesh,
A crown of thorns on his head,
Christ is crucified.
Through the pain and grief,
He bore for all humanity,
Jesus was crucified.
The cross stands empty,
A symbol of sacrificial love,
Christ was crucified.

Anthem

Land of the free skies
Proud anthem that boldly flies
Red, white, blue sunrise
Rising o'er the land
Anthem of the brave and strong
Heard from sea to strand
Freedom rings with might
Anthem's sweet, resounding voice
Echoes through the night

It Never Ends

Eternal cycle
Days blend into one another
Endless repetition
The circle of life
Birth to death and back again
Infinity's grasp
The sun rises, sets
Dawn follows twilight, always
Endless, timeless flow

Don't Go

Please don't go away,
My heart aches with your absence.
Stay, just a bit more.
Don't go, stay with me.
The world outside can wait, love.
Let's cherish this moment.
The night's too lonely,
without you by my side, dear.
Please don't leave me now.

Home Sweet Home

A dog barks inside,
Warm fireplace aglow at night,
Peaceful tales unfold.
A porch swing creaks low,
Crickets trumpet a soft song,
Lemonade in hand.
A place of refuge,
Memories old and yet new,
Where the heart finds rest.

Visions

Dreams become visions
Guiding our path through unknown
Hope and light ahead
Wispy apparitions
Forming images for us
Fleeting like the wind
Eyes closed, we see more
Visions beyond our senses
Opens up our hearts

Blacklist

A shadowy name
Tainted by the blacklist stain
Silenced and afraid
Invisible lines
Dividing the trusted few
Rejected by fear
Blacklisted for words
That stir the righteous anger
The silenced still speak

Blessed With A Curse

Blessed with a curse,
My heart aches for what I crave,
Lonely and confused.
A gift that all want,
A burden I must carry,
Strength in my weakness.
Tears fall from my eyes,
My curse a blessing in sight,
Endless love I give.

Feel My Heart

My heart beats for you,
Its rhythm sings a love song,
Feel my pulse, my dear.
Emotions fill me,
Your touch ignites a fire,
Heart dancing with joy.
In your gentle grasp,
My heart skips a happy beat,
Love flows between us.

Chasing Rainbows

Chasing rainbows bright,
Colors fade as I draw near,
A mirage of hope.
Raindrops and sunshine,
A ribbon in the blue sky,
Elusive beauty.
Run towards the end,
A multicolored canvas,
Treasure in the mist.

Doomed

Doomed by our own greed
The end looming overhead
Nature's revenge lurks
The path we chose led
To a fate we can't escape
Doomed, we march ahead
Folly and hubris
Humanity's fatal flaws
Doomed to repeat them

True Friends

Sunshine or shadow,
True friends stay through it all,
Lifting each other.
Laughter and tears shed,
Heart-to-heart, words unspoken,
True friends understand.
Distance cannot break,
True friends, forever bonded,
Love knows no limits.

Follow You

Footprints in the sand,
I will follow you always,
Guided by your love.
Through the winding streets,
I will chase after your steps,
Till the end of time.
With each beating heart,
I will walk by your side, dear
Until the last breath.

Drown

Gasping for air,
Water fills my lungs and soul,
Peaceful surrender.
Dark depths below me,
Silence of the abyss calls,
My heart beats no more.
Life ebbs away fast,
In the cold embrace of waves,
Drowning, but at peace.

Blasphemy

Blasphemy
Against the divine
Humanity's audacity
Gods above scoffing
Mortals speak in arrogance
Sacredness undone
Rage of worshippers
To those who dare blaspheme
Sins unforgiven

Apologize

Regret fills my heart,
I am sorry, please forgive,
Let us make amends.
Words I must confess,
Mistakes made, actions uncouth,
Forgiveness I plead.
My humble sorry,
May it soothe your wounded heart,
Let peace reign once more.

In The Dark

Walls whisper secrets
Shadows stretch like wounded cats
In the dark, I wait
Silence all around
I strain to hear my own breath
In the dark, I'm lost
Moon casts eerie glow
Ghosts dance in the shadows' depths
In the dark, fear grows

Wonderful Life

Blessed mornings start
Birds chirp, flowers bloom, new day
Nature's gift in sight
Friends and family
Love, laughter, memories made
Happiness within
Full moon, starry night
Peaceful silence, calm surrounds
Contentment prevails

Medicine

Bitter pill to take,
But it brings a swift relief,
Medicine's magic.
Serums and syrups,
Doctors brave the illnesses,
Healing hands at work.
Pain, ache and disease,
Medicine brings a rescue,
Life's precious treasure.

Parasite

Sucking my life force,
Parasite, you drain me dry,
Leave me empty, frail.
Tiny tick latches,
To my skin, drinks my blood, feeds,
Leaves behind disease.
Unseen but deadly,
Parasite hidden inside,
Grows and takes control.

Teardrops

Crystal teardrops fall
Silent whispers of sorrow
Hope for tomorrow
Glistening and pure
Emotions too much to bear
Heartache stains the cheek
A teardrop's journey
From eyes to melancholy
A raindrop of grief

Answers

Eagerly we ask,
Answers come in due time, sweet
Savor each insight.
Mysteries unfold,
With answers a longing quelled,
A peace like no other.
The answer within,
Listen to your inner soul,
It will guide you best.

Christmas

Twinkling lights shine bright
Excitement fills the air tonight
Christmas is all right
Snowflakes dance around
Families gather, cheer sounds
Peace on earth abounds
Presents wrapped with care
Love and joy we all will share
Merry Christmas, so rare

Solitude

In the still silence,
Solitude wraps me tightly,
My soul finds solace.
Alone with my thoughts,
Embraced by sweet serenity,
Peaceful solitude.
Solitude beckons,
A chance to embrace oneself,
Freedom in stillness.

Sentence

Restricted by words,
The sentence brings clarity,
A story unfolds.
Seventeen syllables,
Condensed but powerful words,
A haiku sentence.
Period ends the thought,
A pause before the next one,
Sentence is complete.

Salvation

Drowning, sinking fast
Grace extends a simple hand
Salvation is found
Lost and wandering
A light shines in the distance
Path to salvation
Beneath weight of sin
Wounded, broken, barely alive
Salvation calls out

Escape

Eerie silence reigns,
Fleeing from the mundane life,
Freedom from the chains.
Birds spread their wings wide,
Into the sky they take flight,
Escape, pure delight.
Ditching reality,
Running towards the sunrise,
Breaking free in glee.

Revive

Fluttering eyelids,
As life is breathed back into
Revive the spirit.
Awaken once more,
To the vibrant world around,
Revive thy senses.
From the ashes rise,
Burning with renewed vigor,
Revive the Phoenix.

Survivor

Against all the odds
Survivor fights for life's chance
Strength comes from within
Enduring the storms
Survivor emerges strong
Rays of hope, renewed
The past disintegrated
Survivor rises anew
Count every blessing

Gloom

Dark clouds looming high,
Gloom spreads through the misty sky,
Raindrops start to cry.
Autumn leaves fall down,
Gloomy air all around,
Desolate, no sound.
Foggy, cold and drear,
Melancholy in the air,
Gloom whispers, "I'm here."

Rumors

Whispered words go 'round
Spreading like wildfire does
Truth lost in the flames
Gossip in the breeze
Buzzing like a thousand bees
Lies in every leaf
Rumors twist and turn
Broken records in my mind
Echoes of untruths

First Sight

In crowded spaces,
Our eyes unexpectedly meet,
Heartbeats become one.
On a misty morn,
Silhouettes come into view,
Love at first sunrise.
Across the crowded bar,
Our eyes lock, time stands still now,
Two souls unite souls.

War

Dark clouds of conflict
Smoke and fire rise to sky
Peaceful lives destroyed
Soldiers march in line
Foes ready for the battle
Life or death awaits
War's destruction reigns
Pain and sorrow fill the heart
Hope for peace still lives

Prayers

Hands clasped in prayer,
Hearts yearning for mercy's grace.
Faith, hope, love abide.
Whispered words of hope,
Strength rising from humble pleas.
Prayers heard and answered.
In darkest of times,
Prayers bring light and healing balm.
Hope springs eternal.

Black And Blue

Bruised and battered,
My skin a canvas of pain,
Black and blue my soul.
A touch so gentle,
Yet leaves a mark that lingers,
Black and blue again.
The storm rages on,
The colors merge and blur,
Black and blue the sky.

In Heart

A heart beats within,
Pumping lifeblood through my veins,
Guiding my journey.
Love fills my heart up,
Overflowing with passion,
Emotions abound.
Sadness grips my heart,
Cold and heavy like stone,
Hope brings warmth once more.

Celestial Mechanics

Planetary dance,
Gravity moves them in sync,
Cosmic choreography.
Comet blazing by,
Tugging at the Sun's gravity,
Eccentric orbit.
Saturn's rings aglow,
Moons spin with celestial grace,
A dance in the void.

Supernova

Exploding star's light,
In brilliance, outshining sun,
Supernova bound.
Radiant display,
Fiery waves of cosmic death,
Gone in final burst.
Dazzling supernova,
Eternal legacy shines,
Glowing through the void.

Stellar

Twinkling stars above
Cosmic beauty fills the sky
Stellar dreams ignite
Radiant and bright
Celestial light shining loud
A stellar wonder
Infinite beauty
Stars dance in galactic voids
Stellar masterpiece

Numb

Numbness creeps within,
Suffocating my senses.
Lost in nothingness.
A heart of stone forms,
Shielding me from pain and love.
Numbness takes control.
Frost bites at my skin,
Numbness spreads with every breath.
Winter's icy grip.

Nightfall

The day is fading,
Sunsets paint the many trees
Nightfall draws near.
The stars twinkle bright,
Moonlight cast like a soft glow,
Beauty fills the night.
Silence of the night,
Nature rests as the moon shines,
Darkness brings its peace.

Forlorn

Windswept and lonely,
Forsaken by all who knew,
A heart left to weep.
The forlorn willow,
Bows under weight of sorrow,
Tears falling like rain.
A lone bird's sad song,
Echoes through the silent woods,
Longing for a friend.

Termination

The end has arrived,
Closing of a chapter book,
Time to start anew.
Goodbyes are hard, true,
But the future needs to bloom,
To move forward too.
Termination brings,
The chance for a brand new start,
Hope within new wings.

www.ingramcontent.com/pod-product-compliance
Lightning Source LLC
Chambersburg PA
CBHW051248160726
47994CB00003B/1067